ARIZONA EDIBLE WILD PLANTS FORAGING

Your Guide to Harvesting and Utilizing Wild Edibles and Medicinal Plants in The Grand Canyon State

Edward M Rinaldi

TABLE OF CONTENTS

INTRODUCTION

Arizona, a state known for its dramatic scenery and enthralling deserts, has an equally captivating and varied biodiversity. We dive into the core of this amazing diversity in the first few pages of our investigation into Arizona's edible wild plants, laying the groundwork for an investigation into the practice and philosophy of foraging.

Arizona's Rich Biodiversity

Arizona is a beautiful example of how adaptable nature can be. The state is a canvas covered in a variety of flora, from the recognizable saguaro cacti standing tall in the Sonoran Desert to the delicate blossoms of wildflowers scattered across the high plateaus. An astounding diversity of plant life can be found in the varied ecosystems, which range from low deserts to mountainous terrains.

Foragers need to comprehend this intricate web of biodiversity. There are distinct species in every part of Arizona, each with its traits, applications, and difficulties. The profusion of edible wild plants is a reflection of both the delicate balance found in these ecosystems and the generosity of nature. This section invites readers to explore the complex world of Arizona's flora and to recognize the small details that make each plant an important component of the larger ecological picture.

Art and Science of Foraging

Foraging is a long-standing custom that has been passed down through the generations as well as a science that fosters a close relationship between humans and nature. This science and art take on a unique flavor in Arizona because of the state's arid landscapes and the tenacious plants that inhabit them.

Taking up foraging as a hobby requires accepting a sensory experience. It requires close attention to detail, training your senses to recognize the hues, smells, and textures that distinguish the edible gems concealed in plain sight. An experienced forager gains the ability to read the terrain, recognizing the subtle signs that indicate the presence of nutrient-dense plants just waiting to be found.

However, foraging is more than just a pastime. It is a science-based on understanding and deference. This section highlights how crucial it is to comprehend plant anatomy and terminology so that foragers can make wise choices. Understanding the essential characteristics for identification turns into a compass that leads enthusiasts through Arizona's extensive botanical tapestry. In addition, the section clarifies common lookalikes and potential hazards and suggests a cautious approach to guarantee a secure foraging experience.

The science and art of foraging coexist in harmony, generating a synergy that enables people to make sustainable contributions to their well-being while also fostering a deep connection with nature. Gaining expertise in this art and science opens doors to a world of gastronomic and ecological delights in Arizona, where the stunning desert landscape hides an abundance of edible treasures.

Let the diversity of Arizona's wildlife and the intricate dance of foraging's art and science serve as our beacons as we set out on this journey. Through this exploration, we feed our bodies and develop a profound understanding of the delicate equilibrium that keeps Arizona's wild landscapes intact.

CHAPTER ONE

How to Begin in Arizona

With its wide range of landscapes, Arizona welcomes foragers into a world where success and enjoyment depend on knowing the subtleties of the climate and terrain. This section provides a thorough overview of the climate and landscapes that influence the foraging journey, laying the foundation for going into the wild.

Overview of the Climate and Landscape

Arizona's topography and climate combine to create unique ecosystems that are home to a wide variety of delectable treasures. Every region offers a different foraging experience, from the cool mountain breezes of the Kaibab Plateau to the intense heat of the Sonoran Desert.

The state's southern region is home to the iconic saguaro cactus and parched conditions of the Sonoran Desert. Navigating this terrain as foragers requires them to adjust to the high temperatures and welcome the unique adaptations of plants that flourish in this hostile environment. It becomes important to know the cycles of the desert seasons because some edible plants thrive in short bursts of rain, providing a transient oasis of plenty.

The landscapes change dramatically as one moves north. With its imposing canyons and high deserts, the Colorado Plateau offers foragers a new range of opportunities and difficulties. Here, where elevation greatly influences the variety of plants, pinyon pine nuts, juniper berries, and various wild greens become staples.

The varied vegetation and milder temperatures in mountainous areas like the White Mountains and

Mogollon Rim present a plethora of culinary opportunities for those venturing there. Foragers will find a diverse range of berries, mushrooms, and hearty greens here, all of which add to a culinary mosaic that is a reflection of the region's altitude and climate.

To successfully go on a foraging expedition in Arizona, prospective foragers need to arm themselves with a comprehensive knowledge of the state's diverse climates and topography. This section acts as a compass, helping people navigate the particular difficulties presented by the heat of the Sonoran Desert, the elevation of the high plateaus, and the moderate climate of the mountainous regions.

Equipped with an understanding of the climate and topography of the state, we embrace the diversity that makes every foraging expedition in Arizona unique. Feeling the pulse of Arizona's diverse ecosystems is the first step in the journey from the sun-drenched deserts to the cool mountain air.

Crucial Foraging Equipment for Dry Environments

Arizona's dry landscape necessitates the use of a few basic tools, each with a distinct function in the forager's toolbox. These are not only tools; they are partners in the search for consumable treasures, increasing productivity and security.

1. Foraging Knife: The versatile partner of the forager is a sturdy foraging knife. It is useful for harvesting plants, cutting through tough stems, and preparing gathered edibles because of its sturdy construction and sharp blade. Accuracy is essential, and a high-quality foraging knife guarantees that you will not harm the nearby flora too much.

2. Basket or Bag: Although it may seem basic, a well-made basket or bag is essential to effective foraging. It gives the harvest of the day a place to be stored while allowing air circulation to keep it from wilting. To keep the gathered plants intact and fresh, choose a material that breathes well.

3. Field Guide: When it comes to foraging, information is power, and an extensive field guide that is tailored to Arizona's flora is an essential tool. By offering

information on edibility, applications, and possible lookalikes, it facilitates plant identification. For easy access, pick a guide with concise text and clear illustrations.

4. Water and Hydration System: Due to Arizona's dry climate, regular hydration is necessary. Make sure you stay hydrated during your foraging expedition by packing a durable water bottle or hydration system. In the sweltering desert heat, it serves as more than just a tool.

5. Hand Lens or Magnifying Glass: Details are important in the complex world of foraging. Accurate plant identification is aided by a closer examination of plant features made possible by a hand lens or magnifying glass. This is a very useful tool for differentiating between species that look alike.

6. Gloves: It's important to protect your hands, particularly when working with spiky or thorny plants. Strong gloves protect from scratches and possible allergens, making foraging more comfortable.

A forager's toolkit is built around these fundamental items, which make it easier to navigate Arizona's dry landscape. Every item has a specific function that adds to the effectiveness and success of the foraging project.

Safety Measures to Take Into Account

In addition to having the appropriate equipment, foraging in Arizona's varied landscapes calls for careful attention to safety precautions. When foragers become fully committed to finding wild edibles, these safety measures become essential for a responsible and pleasurable foraging experience.

1. Recognize Your Limits: The landscape of Arizona can be difficult, with hot deserts and steep canyons. Recognize your physical limitations and make realistic plans for your foraging expedition. Make sure you are physically and mentally capable of handling the unique challenges presented by the foraging site you have selected.

2. Protective Clothes: Adequate attire is a means of ensuring safety. Put on long sleeves and pants to shield yourself from the sun, insects, and prickly plants. Sunglasses and a wide-brimmed hat offer more defense against the scorching Arizona sun.

3. Be Aware of Snakes: It's possible to come across snakes in arid areas. When entering places with poor visibility, exercise caution, remain alert, and pay close attention to where you step. Learn about common snake species and their environments.

4. Leave No Trace: Be mindful of the fragile ecosystems of Arizona. Steer carefully to reduce your impact and steer clear of stepping on delicate plants. By only taking what you need and leaving the rest untouched, you can engage in ethical foraging.

5. Keep Up With the Weather: The weather in Arizona can be erratic. Before leaving, pay attention to the weather forecast and be ready for any unexpected changes. Bring extra clothing in case it starts to rain or gets chilly at night.

You can safeguard yourself and help maintain Arizona's natural beauty by including these safety measures and considerations in your foraging practices. Allow responsibility and awareness to lead the way as we set out on this foraging expedition through the breathtaking scenery of the Grand Canyon State.

CHAPTER TWO

Identifying Arizona Flora

A basic understanding of plant anatomy and terminology is necessary before embarking on a foraging adventure in Arizona. We explore the complexities of botanical knowledge in this section, equipping foragers with the knowledge and skills necessary to recognize the wide variety of plants that adorn the state's landscapes.

Terminology and Anatomy of Plants

A solid understanding of plant anatomy is essential for successful foraging. Let's examine some important botanical terms and their meanings:

1. The main organs of photosynthesis are leaves, which are found in a variety of sizes and forms. Take note of the margins, venation patterns, and leaf arrangement. Serrated edges or an opposite leaf arrangement, for instance, can be important indicators of identification.

2. Stems: Plants' support structures, and stems come in a variety of shapes. Woody and herbaceous varieties are possible. Take note of the texture, color, and branching or single nature of the stems.

3. Even though a plant's roots are frequently hidden, they can reveal important information about its identity. Common types include rhizomes, fibrous roots, and taproots. Knowing about root systems makes it easier to identify between various species.

4. Flowers: A plant's reproductive organ, flowers are a treasure trove of data. Observe the color, arrangement, and presence of distinct features such as bracts or spurs on the petals. The quantity of floral parts and flowering patterns are also crucial for identification.

5. Fruits: The fully developed ovary of a flower, which differ greatly in size, shape, and composition. Note whether berries, capsules, nuts, or other fruit varieties are produced by the plant. Essential clues for identifying a species are frequently found in the fruit.

6. Seeds: Studying seeds reveals information about a plant's reproductive tactics. Examine the seed's dimensions, form, and methods of dispersal. While some seeds rely on animals for dispersal, others may have specific adaptations for the wind.

7. Bark: The bark of woody plants can have a noticeable pattern. Observe its color, texture, and any distinctive characteristics, such as peeling or exfoliating bark. Features of the bark are particularly helpful in differentiating between trees and shrubs.

8. Meristem Types: Identification of growth patterns is aided by knowledge of the different types of meristems, or regions of active cell division. Lateral meristems contribute to width, while apical meristems, which are present at the tips of stems, encourage vertical growth.

9. Terminology: Learn words related to plants, such as pinnate venation, compound leaves, and alternate arrangement. Having a firm grasp of terminology makes

it easier to understand field guides and interact with other foragers.

Through studying the anatomy and lexicon of plants, foragers in Arizona arm themselves with the knowledge necessary to traverse the state's varied terrain. This information acts as a compass, helping enthusiasts navigate the fine distinctions between different species, and enhancing the Grand Canyon State's foraging experience.

Crucial Characteristics for Recognition

Understanding Arizona's varied flora requires a careful examination of key characteristics, each of which offers crucial hints for differentiating one plant from another. Let's explore these characteristics in more detail and discover the minute elements that turn a foraging trip into a botanical exploration.

Leaves:
A plethora of information can be gleaned from leaf morphology. Think about how they are arranged on the stem as well as their shape. Identifying characteristics include serrated edges, lobed margins, compound leaves, and simple leaves. The identification process is further

enhanced by noting the presence of hairs, stipules, or glands on the leaf surface.

Flowers:
One of the most fascinating aspects of plant identification is the floral display. Examine the arrangement of petals, sepals, and reproductive organs in addition to colors and shapes. Count the floral parts, take note of the flower's symmetry, and look for any distinctive characteristics, such as spurs or specialized bracts. Identification is further improved by knowledge of the inflorescence type.

Fruits:
A plant's mature fruits offer important information. Examine the fruit to determine if it is a drupe, berry, capsule, nut, or other type. Think about its dimensions, form, and any distinguishing features, like hairs or spines. Having a thorough understanding of the fruit's seed dispersal aids in the identification process.

Bark:
The bark of woody plants becomes a trustworthy identifier. Examine closely its hue, feel, and any distinctive patterns or characteristics. While some trees have distinct lenticels, others have bark that peels off. Features of a plant's bark provide information about its

ecological adaptations in addition to helping with identification.

General Growth Form:
Step back and examine the general growth form of the plant. Is it a ground-hugging herb, a towering tree, or a shrub? Knowing forms and growth habits helps focus options, especially when paired with other characteristics like leaves and flowers.

Microhabitats and Habitats:
Plants frequently exhibit preferences for particular microhabitats or habitats. The identification process is aided by environmental indicators such as riparian zones, rocky slopes, and sandy soil. Take note of the surrounding vegetation and soil conditions; they offer important background information.

Seasonal Variations
The appearance of a plant can change with the seasons. Fruits may ripen and spread, leaves may change color, and flowers may bloom and then wither. Plant life cycle observation improves identification precision and strengthens the forager's bond with the organic rhythms of Arizona's landscapes.

Foragers in Arizona take on a journey that goes beyond the simple pursuit of edibles by focusing on these essential characteristics and accepting the complexities of plant identification. It turns into an investigation of the distinctive botanical tapestry that threads through the canyons, mountains, and deserts, elevating every foraging adventure into a celebration of the diversity of nature.

Frequently Occurring Lookalikes and Pitfalls in the Arizona Desert

Foragers must avoid potential hazards and be mindful of lookalike plants to ensure a safe and enjoyable experience, even though the vast landscapes of the Arizona desert offer a bounty of edible treasures. Foraging becomes more cautious when one is aware of these typical traps.

1. Death Camas vs. Lupine:
Together with the poisonous Death Camas, lupine grows bright spikes of flowers in the parched landscape. Their long, narrow leaves are similar, making identification difficult. One of the distinguishing characteristics is that Death Camas lacks a stem, whereas Lupine has one. It's important to use caution because mistaking Death Camas for Lupine can have dangerous outcomes.

2. Ragwort versus Desert Marigold:

Although Ragwort's vivid yellow blooms are similar to those of Desert Marigold, Ragwort is poisonous due to its alkaloids. Different leaf shapes and arrangements can be seen upon closer inspection. The leaves of Ragwort are more elongated and toothed than those of Desert Marigold, which have deeply lobed leaves. Precise identification stops harmful plants from being accidentally consumed.

3. Claret Cup Cactus versus Hedgehog Cactus:

Claret Cup Cacti and Hedgehog Cacti both have eye-catching red flowers that could be confusing. Their general appearance and supination, however, are different. The Claret Cup Cactus has fewer, more densely packed spines than the Hedgehog Cactus, which has a more pronounced central spine. With careful observation, foragers can take in the beauty without running into any danger.

4. Jimsonweed vs. Prickly Pear:

Common and edible cactus called prickly pear is sometimes confused with the toxic plant Jimsonweed. Although their leaves resemble paddles, Prickly Pears have spines and a unique structure. Conversely, jimsonweed has more asymmetrical leaf shapes and is devoid of spines. Making sure people are properly identified helps to avoid poisoning accidents.

5. Yucca versus agave:

Plants that resemble yucca and agave may be confused. Their features vary, though, in terms of leaf structure and arrangement. Yucca leaves cluster along a central stalk, whereas agave leaves are usually arranged in a rosette. By being aware of these differences, foragers can select the most suitable plant to eat.

The botanical landscape of the Arizona desert can be tricky to navigate because of common lookalikes and potential hazards. Equipped with expertise and a dedication to meticulous observation, foragers can convert possible dangers into chances for a more secure and rewarding encounter with the distinctive vegetation of the Grand Canyon State.

CHAPTER THREE

Arizona Foraging Locations

To truly discover Arizona's edible treasures, one must venture into the state's many ecosystems. We untangle the web of ecosystems in this section, each providing a distinct foraging opportunity. Knowing these ecosystems gives foragers looking to find delicious food in Arizona's diverse landscapes a road map.

The State's Ecosystems

1. Desert of Sonora:
Renowned for its unique flora and harsh temperatures, the Sonoran Desert stretches across southern Arizona. In this area, foragers come across a variety of drought-resistant plants, the prickly pear, and towering saguaro cacti. The dry conditions of the desert necessitate a keen sense of seasonal variations and the ability to recognize hardy edibles that have adapted to this difficult setting.

2. Mojave Desert:
Foragers face new difficulties and opportunities as the Mojave Desert spreads into Arizona's northwest corner. A variety of yucca species, creosote bushes, and Joshua trees can be found in this desert area. To survive in the high-desert environment of the Mojave Desert, foragers must adjust to the limited vegetation and special adaptations of the plants.

3. Chaparral
The Chaparral ecosystem connects the desert and the forest; it is located in the central and southeast regions. Foragers make their way among prickly bushes, fragrant herbs, and a variety of plants. A variety of edible species are introduced in this transitional zone, such as

manzanita berries, wild rose hips, and various herbs. Foraging successfully requires an understanding of how arid and woodland conditions interact.

4. Pine-Oak Forest:
Foragers ascend higher altitudes to reach the Pine-Oak Woodland ecosystems that are characteristic of central and eastern Arizona's mountainous regions. Rich foraging grounds are provided by ponderosa pines, oak trees, and a variety of undergrowth. In contrast to the dry lowlands, pine nuts, edible mushrooms, and a variety of berries emerge as prominent features.

5. Zones for Riparians:
The flowing water that characterizes Arizona's riparian zones creates a lush environment full of edible opportunities. Foragers find watercress, wild berries, and other plants that require moisture along rivers and streams. These desert oases highlight the variety of experiences that come with foraging near water.

6. Elevated alpine forests:
Traveling to the top of the White Mountains and other high places reveals high alpine forests. Tightly packed with aspens, conifers, and a profusion of underbrush, these forests offer a forager's dream come true. In the cool, mountainous air, edible mushrooms, berries, and a variety of greens flourish.

To successfully navigate these ecosystems, one must be flexible and have a deep awareness of the distinctive qualities of each location. In Arizona, foragers are doing more than just exploring new terrain; they are taking a culinary tour of the many fascinating ecosystems that contribute to the state's unique culinary character.

Arizona's Best Foraging Seasons

In Arizona, foraging is a dynamic activity because the availability of edible plants varies greatly with the seasons. With new opportunities and factors to consider with every season, foragers are presented with a year-round rich tapestry of flavors.

- **Springtime:**

In Arizona, springtime is a forager's delight. The landscape is changed by the occasional burst of growth brought on by the cooler temperatures and rainfall. Many kinds of wildflowers bloom at this time of year, creating a visual spectacle as well as delicious treats. Seek out desert marigolds, prickly pear blossoms, and the tender shoots of various wild greens. The vibrant foraging experience is enhanced by the presence of pollinators, who are drawn to the abundance of floral resources.

- **Summertime:**

Foragers in Arizona deal with the extreme heat during the summer months. But there are unique culinary opportunities this season offers. Fruits and flowers can be found on desert-adapted plants like saguaro cactus and mesquite trees. Particularly mesquite pods mature and become a sweet and nutrient-rich ingredient. Because of the strength of the midday sun, foragers need to schedule their excursions during the cooler hours of the day.

- **Monsoon Season:**

The dry landscapes receive a sudden infusion of moisture when the monsoon season arrives in late summer. Several plants respond to this, which starts a second wave of growth. It is anticipated by foragers that some wild greens, mushrooms, and late-season fruits will become more accessible. But, timing must be carefully considered, as unexpected downpours can make conditions difficult in some areas.

- **Autumn:**

Fall is the best time of year to go foraging in Arizona because it brings with it a return to milder temperatures. Many desert plants ripen their fruits during this time, providing a wide variety of flavors. A rich harvest is produced by the appearance of juniper berries, acorns, and prickly pear fruits. Foraging excursions are made more visually appealing by the changing foliage and the more comfortable exploration made possible by the cooler weather.

- **Winter:**

Even though Arizona's winters are generally mild, foragers can still come across delicious treasures. Some desert plants provide their leaves as a resource, such as yucca and agave. Furthermore, fruits from hardier species may still be produced at lower elevations. Foragers should plan for and be ready for lower temperatures, particularly in higher elevations.

To successfully forage in Arizona, one must comprehend the subtle differences between each season. It entails identifying the edible offerings as well as adjusting to the difficulties brought about by the state's various climates. Foragers in Arizona uncover a culinary calendar that honors the constantly shifting bounty of the Grand Canyon State by aligning with the rhythm of the state's seasons.

Laws, Licenses, and Ethical Foraging Methods

Maintaining moral and legal standards is necessary when foraging in Arizona's varied landscapes. A sustainable and pleasurable foraging experience depends on knowing the rules, getting permits when needed, and engaging in respectful foraging practices.

Rules:

Learn about local and state laws about the collection of plants before setting out on a foraging expedition. Restrictions may be in place in some areas to safeguard delicate ecosystems or endangered species. There are frequently rules specific to state and national parks, wildlife preserves, and tribal lands. To remain up to date and prevent unintentionally breaking any regulations, check with the appropriate authorities.

Licenses:

Permissions may occasionally be needed to go foraging in particular locations. There may be permit systems in place for national forests, state parks, or tribal lands to control and regulate foraging activities. Obtaining the required permits supports responsible land management practices, which supports conservation efforts in addition to ensuring compliance with regulations.

Appropriate Foraging Techniques:

Ethical foraging requires us to respect the environment and the communities that live there. A harmonious relationship between foragers and the ecosystems they investigate can be fostered by implementing the following practices:

1. Leave No Trace: Reduce your impact by abiding by the guidelines of this policy. Refrain from littering, stay on designated trails, and don't step on delicate vegetation. Save the landscape's natural splendor for upcoming foragers.

Harvest responsibly by taking only what you require and leaving the remaining food unaltered. Overharvesting can upset the equilibrium of nearby ecosystems and hurt plant populations. The sustainability of wild edibles is ensured through selective and thoughtful harvesting.

2. Cultural Respect: Indigenous communities may attach cultural significance to certain locations. Respect regional customs and refrain from foraging in places that are sacred or delicately culturally associated. When in doubt, get permission, and keep in mind the customs of the local people.

3. Educate Yourself: Keep learning about the ethics of foraging and the local flora. Keep abreast of

conservation initiatives and best practices. You can be sure that your foraging practices follow the most recent conservation guidelines by continuing your education.

Foragers help to protect Arizona's biodiversity and natural beauty by following rules, getting permits when needed, and engaging in ethical foraging practices. Responsible foraging guarantees a sustainable harvest and strengthens ties to the communities and landscapes that distinguish Grand Canyon State as a special place to go foraging.

CHAPTER FOUR

Arizona's Edible Plants

Fruits and Berries

1. Prickly pears
(Pointia spp.)

- Where to Find It: Found all over the state, but particularly in the Sonoran Desert.
- Best Time to Forage: When the tunas ripen, which is in late spring or early summer.
- How to Forage: Gather the tunas using gloves or tongs, being careful not to snag on spines. Enjoy the juicy, sweet flesh after peeling.

- Description: The flat, paddle-like stems of prickly pear cacti are their distinguishing feature. The hues of the fruits range from red to purple.

2. Juniper Berry
(Juniperus spp)

- Location: Usually found in higher altitudes, like the Pine-Oak Woodland.
- Best Time to Forage: When berries are fully ripe, late summer to fall.

- How to Forage: Gather the purple to blueberries, which are frequently used as a spice in food preparation.
- Description: Aromatic juniper bushes have leaves that resemble needles. The berries taste strongly of resin.

3. Manzanita
(Arctostaphylos spp.)

- Where to Look: Chaparral areas, frequently at higher altitudes.
- When to Forage: As the berries ripen, in late summer or early fall.

- How to Forage: Collect the tiny reddish-orange berries and use them dried or fresh in jams and tea.
- Description: Oval-shaped leaves and smooth, reddish bark characterize manzanita bushes.

4. Elderberry
(Sambucus spp.)

Where to Look: In mountainous and riverine regions.
- Best Time to Forage: When clusters of dark purple berries appear, which is in late summer or early fall.

- How to Forage: Gather ripe berries and use them in jams, syrups, and dessert recipes.
- Description: Elderberry shrubs yield small berries in umbrella-like clusters and have compound leaves.

- How to Forage: Gather the feathery plumes that hold tiny fruits, then use them as a spice or in teas.
- Description: Apache Plume is a shrub that has unique plumes and leaves that are a silvery gray color.

5. Apache Plume
(The Fallugia paradoxa)

- Where to Find It: Dry areas, like the Sonoran Desert.
- When to Forage: When the pinkish-white plumes appear, which is in late spring or early summer.

6. Cowberry
(Shepherdia species)

- Where to Find: Found in a range of environments, including hilly areas.
- When to Forage: When the red or orange berries are ripe, which is in late summer to early fall.

- How to Forage: Gather the berries to use in jellies, jams, or as a tart garnish for food.
- Description: The branches of buffaloberry shrubs are prickly and have silvery leaves.

7. Chokecherry
(Prunus virginiana)

- Where to Look: Higher elevations and riverine regions.
- When to Forage: In late summer, when the cherries turn from dark purple to black.
- How to Forage: Gather ripe cherries and remove the pits to use in jams, syrups, or desserts.
- Description: Chokecherry trees bear clusters of tiny cherries and have serrated leaves.

8. Currant
(family Ribes)

- Where to Find: Riparian zones and mountainous areas.
- Best Time to Forage: When clusters of red, black, or white berries emerge in late spring or early summer.
- How to Forage: Gather the berries to make jams, desserts, or fresh eating.

- Description: Currant bushes produce tiny, translucent berries and have lobed leaves.

9. Serviceberry
(Amelanchier spp.)

- Where to Find: Mountainous areas and higher elevations.
- Best Time to Forage: When berry clusters ripen, which is in late spring or early summer.
- How to Forage: Collect berries for baking, jams, or fresh consumption.
- Description: Sweet, blue-purple berries are produced by serviceberry shrubs or small trees, which have ovate leaves.

10. Fruit of Yucca
(Yucca spp.)

- Where to Look: Arid regions, such as chaparral and deserts.
- When to Forage: As the big, juicy fruits ripen, which is in late spring or early summer.
- How to Forage: Gather the ripe fruits, take out the seeds, and use them as an ingredient in recipes or salads.
- Description: Yucca plants are distinguished by their distinctive fruits that follow tall spikes of

creamy-white   flowers   and   long,   sword-like
                                  leaves.

Discovering these delicious fruits and berries throughout
Arizona's diverse landscapes is a way to connect with the
state's abundant natural resources while also embarking
on a gastronomic journey.

Herbs and Wild Greens

1. Dandelion
(Taraxacum officinale)

- Where to Find It: Found in a variety of environments, such as open fields, meadows, and lawns.
- When to Forage: When leaves are tender, from early spring to late fall.
- How to Forage: Cook mature leaves as greens or gather young leaves for salads. You can eat the entire plant.

2. Nettle
(Urtica spp.)

- Where to Look: Shaded, damp spots that are frequently close to water sources.
- When to Forage: Early in the spring, when new shoots appear.
- How to Forage: Blanch or cook nettles to add a nutrient-rich component to dishes, but wear gloves to protect your hands from stinging hairs.

3. Lamb's Quarters

(Chenopodium album)

- Location: Usually found in fields, gardens, and disturbed areas.
- When to Forage: During the tender season of spring to early fall.
- How to Forage: Gather tender leaves to add to salads or cook in place of spinach.

4. Wild mustard

(Brassica spp.)

- Where to Look: Fields, disturbed areas, and roadside spots.
- Best Time to Forage: During the flavorful leaves of spring to early summer.
- How to Forage: Gather leaves to use as a spice, in sautés, or salads. Pickled seed pods are another option.

5. Chickweed

(Stellaria media)

Where to Look: Soggy, shaded spots, frequently in gardens or disturbed ground.
- When to Forage: During the spring to

early summer, when there are lots of young shoots.

- How to Forage: Add fresh chickweed as a garnish or use it in salads. It tastes mild with a hint of sweetness.

6. Plantain
(species of Plantago)

- Location: Fields, disturbed areas, and lawns.

The best times to forage are in the spring and early summer, but it's possible all year round.

- How to Forage: Cook mature leaves as greens

or gather young leaves for salads.

7. Mallow
(Malva species)

- Location: Roadside ditches, gardens, and disturbed areas.

- When to Forage: During the tender season of spring to early fall.

- How to Forage: Sauté young leaves as greens or incorporate them into salads. Mallow tastes mild and a little bit mucilaginous.

8. Wild spinach

(Atriplex spp.)

- Where to Find It: Dry areas, particularly those with sandy or alkaline soils.

- Best Time to Forage: In late spring or early summer, when the leaves are still tender and young.

- How to Forage: Gather and sauté leaves to replace spinach. The plant can withstand dry conditions quite well.

9. Oleander woods

(Oxalis spp.)

- Where to Look: Open meadows, forests, and shaded spots.

- Best Time to Forage: In the spring to early fall, when there are lots of leaves.

- How to Forage: Garnish salads with fresh, lemony wood sorrel leaves.

10. Amaranth

(various species)

- Location: Fields, gardens, and disturbed areas.

- When to Forage: While young leaves are tender, in late spring to early autumn.

- Foraging Techniques: Gather and prepare tender leaves as greens. To produce a grain that is high in nutrients, mature plant seeds can be harvested.

Seeds and Nuts

1. Pinyon pine
(Pinus edulis)

- Where to Find It: Higher elevations in the Pine-Oak Woodland.
- When to Forage: When pine nuts reach maturity in late summer or early fall.
- How to Forage: Gather pine nuts from cones and utilize them in a variety of recipes.

2. Juniper
(Juniperus spp.)

- Where to Find It: Pine-Oak Woodland and other habitats.
- When to Forage: As the juniper berries ripen, which is in late summer or early fall.
- Foraging Techniques: Gather the blue to purple berries and utilize them as a spice or medicinal herb.

3. Acorns
(Quercus spp.)

Where to Look: Forests and oak woodlands.

- Fall is the best time to forage when acorns are falling.

- How to Forage: Gather acorns, grind them into flour for a variety of culinary purposes, and remove the tannins.

4. Mesquite
(Prosopis   spp.)

- Where to Look: Dry areas, particularly the Sonoran Desert.

- When to Forage: As the mesquite pods reach maturity in late summer or early fall.

- Foraging Tip: Gather mesquite pods and grind them into a sugary flour for drinks or baking.

5. Chia
(Salvia hispanica)

- Where to Look: Dry areas, frequently with disturbed soils.
- When to Forage: As seeds ripen, in late spring or early summer.
- How to Forage: Gather chia seeds and incorporate them into different recipes to reap their nutritional advantages.

6. Sunflowers
(Heliocentrus species)

- Where to Find It: Open fields and other types of habitat.
- When to Forage: Sunflower seeds mature in late summer particularly in the mountains of the desert.

- How to Forage: Gather pinon nuts from cones and utilize them in cooking.

10. Acacia Seeds

- Where to Look: Dry areas, frequently with disturbed soils.
- When to Forage: As seeds ripen, in late summer or early fall.
- How to Forage: Gather and process acacia seeds into a wholesome flour.

Discovering Arizona's bounty of wild greens, herbs, nuts, and seeds opens up a world of flavor and nutrition that makes foraging into a culinary journey that ties foragers to the natural beauty of the state.

Discover the Benefits of Roots and Tubers

1. Desert mariposa lily
(Calocronus kennedyi)

- Where to Find It: Dry areas with rocky or sandy soils.
- When to Forage: During the growth stage of tubers, which is late spring to early summer.
- Foraging Instructions: Gently extract the tubers, which can be boiled or roasted to make a starchy snack.

2. Yucca
(Yucca   spp.)

- Where to Look: Arid regions, such as chaparral and deserts.
- The best time to forage is in late spring or early summer when the roots are easiest to reach.
- How to Forage: Gather the roots, which can be cooked, peeled, and sliced to add starch and fiber to dishes.

3. Wild onions:
(Allium spp.)

- Where to Find It: Meadows and grasslands, among other habitats.
Foraging Season: Spring, when the bulbs are full of fat.
- How to Forage: Pull up the bulbs and add them to dishes for a strong onion flavor.

4. Wild potatoes
(Solanum jamesii)

- Where to Find: Dry areas with typically sandy soils.
- When to Forage: When tubers are fully developed, which is in late spring or early summer.
- To forage, dig up the tubers; these can be dried or cooked and used later.

5. Camas Lily

(Camassia spp.)

- Where to Find: Meadows and riparian zones are frequently found in mountainous regions.

- When to Forage: When the bulbs are swollen, which is in late spring or early summer.

- Foraging tip: Gather the bulbs and boil them to make a starchy, sweet meal.

6. Groundnut

(Apios americana)

- Where to Find: Riparian areas are frequently found next to rivers or streams.

- When to Forage: When the tubers are mature, which is in late spring or early summer.

- Foraging Instructions: Dig up the tubers, which have a nutty, potato-like flavor when boiled or roasted.

7. Salsify

(Tragopogon porrifolius)

- Where to Find: Disturbed areas, frequent fields or by the sides of roads.

- When to Forage: When the roots are tender, which is in late spring or early summer.

- Foraging tip: Gather the roots, which you can cook or incorporate into stews and soups.

8. Biscuitroot

(Lomatium spp.)

- Where to Find It: Dry areas with rocky or sandy soils.

- When to Forage: When the tubers are plump, which is in late spring or early summer.

- Foraging Method: Pull up the tubers; they make a starchy food source when boiled or roasted.

9.　　　Balsamroot Arrowleaf *(Balsamorhiza sagittata)*

- Location: Grasslands, foothills, and open meadows.
- When to Forage: When the roots are at their peak, which is in late spring or early summer.
- Foraging Techniques: Gather the taproots, which you can dry or roast for later use.

10. Desert parsley *(Lomatium spp.)*

- Where to Find It: Dry areas with rocky or sandy soils.
- When to Forage: When the tubers are fully developed, which is in late spring or early summer.
- Foraging Method: Harvest the tubers by digging them up; they taste similar to cooked sweet potatoes.

Foragers can explore a wide range of starchy and nutrient-dense options by exploring Arizona's tuber and root systems, which enhances and prolongs their culinary investigation of the state's wild edibles.

CHAPTER FIVE

Arizona Flavors

From Desert to Plate: Recipe Preparation Methods

A combination of imagination, skill, and culinary artistry is needed to transform the abundance of wild edibles found in Arizona from barren desert landscapes into mouthwatering dishes. The following cooking methods will improve your foraging experience:

1. Grilling in the desert:
- Technique: Gather juicy, prickly pear pads and toss them in a mixture of herbs, garlic, and olive oil. For a smoky flavor, grill over an open flame. This can be used to make a taco filling or a savory side dish.

2. untamed green pesto:
- Technique: Gather a variety of wild greens, such as lamb's quarters, dandelion, and nettle. To make a tasty pesto, blend them with pine nuts, garlic, Parmesan, and olive oil. Use as a spread for artisan bread or as a topping for pasta.

3. Marinades Infused with Juniper:
- Technique: Add crushed juniper berries to meat or vegetable marinades. The berries enhance the flavor of your grilled or roasted dishes with their distinct flavor profile and fragrant, piney aroma.

4. Elements of Prickly Pears:
- Technique: Pick ripe, prickly pears and squeeze out their colorful juice. Combine with sparkling water, a squeeze of citrus, and a dash of honey to create a cool drink with a desert theme.

5. Baking Mesquite Pod Flour:
- Technique: Finely grind the dried mesquite pods. Blend with regular flour to give bread, muffins, or pancakes a hint of sweetness and nutty flavor.

6. Pickling Cholla Buds:
Technique: Gather young cholla buds and pickle them in a brine made with spices, vinegar, and water. These tart pickled buds are a great garnish for sandwiches, salads, or charcuterie boards.

7. Reduced Wild Berries:
- Trick: Gather a variety of wild berries, including currants, buffaloberries, and elderberries. Reduce them with a little sugar to make colorful, flavorful sauces to pour over desserts or use as a glaze for meats.

8. Soup with Acorn Squash:
- Technique: To get rid of tannins, harvest and prepare acorns. Acorns can be roasted and then blended with

acorn squash to make a creamy soup that tastes hearty and nutty.

9. Yucca Chips:
Technique: Cut the roots of yucca into fries after harvesting them. For a crispy take on classic potato fries, toss with olive oil and your preferred spices, then bake or fry.

10. Delectable Fruit Gel:
- Technique: To make a cool sorbet, take advantage of the sweetness of succulent fruits like saguaro and prickly pears. For a naturally sweet and refreshing dessert, blend the fruits with a dash of lime and place in the freezer.

Try these methods to highlight the distinct flavors of wild edibles in Arizona. Every dish, such as the foraged herb pestos and grilled cactus pads, honors the varied and nourishing ingredients present in the Grand Canyon State's environments.

Recipes to Please Every Taste

Take a culinary tour of Arizona's wild edibles with these varied recipes, which have been thoughtfully created to suit all palates:

1. Salad with Prickly Pears:

Ingredients: Fresh prickly pear pads; cherry tomatoes; feta cheese; mixed wild greens; balsamic vinaigrette.

- Directions: Grill thinly sliced prickly pear pads and combine with crumbled feta, wild greens, and tomatoes. Add a balsamic vinaigrette drizzle for a flavorful and refreshing salad.

2. Tontos de Sonora del Desert:

Ingredients: Salsa verde, cilantro, lime, grilled yucca fries, seasoned shredded wild game or plant-based protein.

- Instructions: To create a distinctive taco with a Sonoran flair, stuff grilled yucca fries with seasoned protein and garnish with salsa verde, cilantro, and lime juice.

3. Venison Skewers Spiced with Juniper:

Cubed venison, crushed juniper berries, garlic, olive oil, rosemary, salt, and pepper are the ingredients.

- Instructions: Marinate garlic, olive oil, rosemary, crushed juniper berries, salt, and pepper in venison. For a fragrant and flavorful dish, skewer and grill.

4. Pancakes made with mesquite:

Ingredients: Maple syrup, mesquite pod flour, and conventional pancake ingredients.

- Instructions: For a nutty and slightly sweet flavor, replace part of the traditional flour with mesquite pod flour. Serve with maple syrup for a tasty morning meal.

5. Fried Cholla Buds:
Ingredients: Fresh cholla buds; mixed vegetables; tofu or desired protein; ginger; garlic; soy sauce.
- Directions: Stir-fry the cholla buds with your favorite protein, tofu, or a medley of vegetables. For a savory dish, season with garlic, ginger, and soy sauce.

6. Wild Berry Pastry:
- Ingredients: Pie crust, sugar, cornstarch, egg wash, and mixed wild berries.
- Instructions: Combine sugar and cornstarch with wild berries. Line a pie crust with the mixture, fold over the edges, and brush with egg wash. For a tasty and rustic wild berry galette, bake.

7. Curry made with Yucca Root:
Ingredients: Tofu or desired meat substitute, vegetables, coconut milk, curry powder, and sliced yucca roots.
- Instructions: Add veggies and protein after simmering yucca roots in coconut milk with curry spices. Serve with rice for a flavorful, filling curry.

8. Thumbprint Cookies with Buffaloberry Jam:

Ingredients: Butter, sugar, flour, vanilla extract, and buffaloberry jam.

- Instructions: To make a delicious sweet treat, press thumbprint cookies, fill the centers with buffaloberry jam, and bake.

9. Bars of Amaranth Energy:

Ingredients: Nuts, honey, nut butter, dried fruits, and amaranth seeds.

- Directions: Combine nut butter, honey, chopped nuts, dried fruits, and amaranth seeds. Press into bars and store in the fridge for a wholesome, high-energy snack.

10. Squash Acorns and Mariposa Lilies in the Desert Soup:

Ingredients: Cream, broth, spices, roasted acorn squash, and desert mariposa lily tubers.

- Instructions: Puree-cooked mariposa lily tubers and roasted acorn squash with spices and broth. To make the soup velvety and flavorful, add cream.

These recipes offer a wide variety of flavors that are sure to please any palate, capturing the essence of Arizona's wild edibles. Every dish, from sweet treats to savory entrees, highlights the distinctive ingredients that can only be found in the Grand Canyon State.

CHAPTER SIX

Conservation and Ethical Foraging Practices

Foraging's Effect on Arizona's Ecosystems

In Arizona's varied landscapes, foraging is a privilege with obligations. It is essential to comprehend how foraging affects the ecosystems of the state to promote moral behavior and long-term environmental partnerships.

1. Preservation of Habitat and Biodiversity:
When foraging is done carelessly, it can endanger Arizona's ecosystems' biodiversity. The delicate balance between flora and fauna can be upset by overharvesting some plant species, which affects the availability of food and shelter for wildlife. Choosing plants for foraging ethically entails allowing them to fulfill their natural life cycle and contribute to the ecosystem's general health.

2. Erosion of Soil and Disturbances:
In delicate habitats, like riparian zones or delicate desert soils, trampling and overharvesting can cause habitat disruption and soil erosion. This may have an impact on native plant growth, encourage the spread of invasive species, and jeopardize the stability of these ecosystems. Reducing these adverse effects is possible by adhering to the Leave No Trace philosophy and paying attention to the terrain.

3. Protection of Endangered Species:
Some plant species in Arizona may be already endangered or threatened. Unintentionally contributing to the decline of these vulnerable species can occur when foraging occurs without the necessary knowledge and awareness. Foragers can help by observing designated protected areas and refraining from collecting endangered species. Conservation efforts should be directed toward safeguarding and maintaining these plants.

4. Introduction to Invasive Species:
To prevent unintentionally bringing invasive species into new areas, foragers should exercise caution. Ecological disruptions may result from seeds or plant material adhering to clothes or tools and being carried to new areas. Native ecosystems are protected in part by routinely cleaning equipment and being mindful of the possible spread of invasive species.

5. Resilience to Climate Change:
The effects of climate change are already being felt by Arizona's ecosystems. To prevent aggravating the stress caused by climate change, foragers should be mindful of the delicate balance that these ecosystems maintain. Ethical foraging methods complement initiatives aimed

at improving adaptability and resilience to changing weather patterns.

Indigenous and Cultural Aspects to Take Into Account:
For indigenous communities in Arizona, a variety of plants are important cultural symbols. Foragers need to recognize and honor the traditional wisdom surrounding these plants. The preservation of the environment and cultural heritage is aided by asking for permission when required and by comprehending and honoring cultural customs.

In summary, it is imperative that foraging in Arizona minimizes adverse effects on the state's diverse ecosystems. A thorough awareness of the relationships between plants, animals, and their environments is necessary for ethical foraging techniques. Foragers help ensure that Arizona's ecosystems remain healthy and beautiful for future generations by adhering to conservation principles.

Conscientious Gathering Methods in the Dry Setting

In Arizona's dry climate, foraging demands careful planning to guarantee sustainability and reduce the disturbance of fragile ecosystems. The following are essential guidelines for ethical foraging in arid areas:

- **Seasonal Sensitivity:**

It is essential to comprehend the seasonality of plant life in arid environments. Numerous plants have distinct growing seasons and are reliant on scarce water supplies. To avoid harvesting during crucial times like drought or intense heat, foragers should time their activities to coincide with the cycles of the natural world.

- **Methods of Mindful Harvesting:**

Minimizing plant stress can be achieved by using gentle harvesting techniques. To protect surrounding vegetation, roots, and stems, foragers should employ the proper equipment and techniques. Plants can regenerate and contribute to the general health of the ecosystem when only what is necessary is taken and the remaining material is left behind.

- **How Not to Overharvest:**

Arizona's arid climate frequently results in slower plant growth and scarce resources. To allow plant populations to recover in between harvests, foragers must exercise caution to avoid overharvesting. Respectful foraging entails removing enough people to maintain the species' viability.

- **Don't Leave Any Traces**:

In dry areas where the ecological balance is vulnerable, it is imperative to follow the Leave No Trace guidelines. Reduce the physical impact by packing out all waste, adhering to designated trails, and avoiding tromping on delicate soils. This guarantees that the foraging activity leaves the landscape with as little lasting impact as possible.

- **Considering Animals and Their Habitats:**

A wide range of wildlife that has evolved to withstand harsh conditions can be found in arid environments. Foragers ought to take care not to disturb or harm wildlife habitats. Encouraging respect for wildlife's natural behavior benefits the ecosystem as a whole.

Teaching and Increasing Consciousness:
Building a community of environmentally conscious foragers requires raising awareness of responsible foraging practices. Education promotes sustainable foraging practices and aids in people's understanding of the particular difficulties faced by arid environments.

Promoting Arizona's Local Biodiversity

In Arizona, preserving local biodiversity requires proactive measures to improve ecosystem resilience and health in addition to ethical foraging techniques. Here are some methods to support biodiversity in your area:

1. Cultivating Native Plants:
Think about growing native plants in your yard or public areas. This promotes local biodiversity and offers educational and appreciative opportunities for Arizona's distinctive flora.

2. Take Part in Restoration Initiatives:
Participate in or lend support to restoration initiatives that preserve native plants. To support biodiversity, these projects frequently entail clearing invasive species, replanting native plants, and repairing habitats.

3. Work Together with Conservation Groups:
Make contact with neighborhood conservation groups that are committed to protecting Arizona's natural resources. Contributions in the form of time or resources can support ongoing initiatives to preserve and restore natural habitats.

4. Encourage the Sustainable Use of Land:
Promote sustainable land use regulations that give the preservation of natural environments top priority. Encourage the implementation of programs that strike a balance between protecting Arizona's many ecosystems and human activity.

5. Conscientious Land Management:
Use responsible land management techniques if you own or manage land in Arizona. This could entail putting in place sustainable farming methods, reducing habitat disturbance, and managing invasive species.

6. Participation in the Community:
Spread the word about the value of biodiversity conservation in your community. Motivate people to embrace actions that reduce their influence on nearby ecosystems and foster an awareness of environmental responsibility.

People can make a significant contribution to protecting Arizona's rich natural heritage for future generations by adopting responsible foraging practices and actively supporting regional biodiversity initiatives.

CONCLUSION

Developing a Long-Term Partnership with Arizona's Wild Harvest

Building a sustainable relationship with wild harvest is more than just a practice in Arizona's vast and varied landscapes; it's a commitment to maintaining the state's ecological richness. It is clear from the end of this investigation into the world of edible plants in Arizona that the transition from forager to steward is one of great importance.

1. Building Biodiversity Respect:
The state of Arizona's biodiversity, a delicate dance of plants and animals that have adapted to the difficulties of arid environments, is demonstrated by the state's wild harvest. The journey we take through this guide emphasizes how important it is to comprehend, honor, and preserve this complex fabric of life.

2. Foraging and Conservation in Balance:
The privilege of foraging is not without responsibility. Our influence on Arizona's ecosystems ought to be balanced, balancing conservation efforts with the hunt for edible wild plants. As stewards of the land, we ensure that our actions positively impact the resilience of these special environments by implementing responsible foraging practices.

3. Preservation and Appreciation of Culture:
It is essential to recognize and value the cultural significance associated with these resources as we delve into the culinary and medicinal treasures of Arizona's wild plants. For many years, indigenous communities have developed a close bond with the land and all it has to offer. Building a long-term relationship with Arizona's wild harvest requires honoring and protecting this cultural legacy.

4. An Appeal for Sustainable Living

More than just a food source, Arizona's wild harvest extends an invitation to a sustainable way of living. The journey doesn't end at the plate—whether it's root and tuber goodness, nourishing greens, or foraging for juicy berries. It encompasses the decisions we make daily regarding how we engage with the environment, maintain regional biodiversity, and enhance ecosystem health.

5. Toward the Future:

Looking forward requires both responsibility and hope as we cultivate a sustainable relationship with Arizona's wild harvest. We become stewards of Arizona's ecological legacy by incorporating ethical foraging practices into our daily lives, guaranteeing that coming generations can continue to enjoy the rich and varied offerings of the Grand Canyon State.

Finally, the exploration of Arizona's edible plants serves as an invitation to live in harmony with nature rather than merely consume it. Let a dedication to sustainability, conservation, and a lasting reverence for the wild harvest that enhances Arizona's landscapes serve as our compass when we go out foraging.

www.ingramcontent.com/pod-product-compliance
Lightning Source LLC
Chambersburg PA
CBHW071053260726
48661CB00006B/2247